BEFORE THE CAMERAS

LEAVE UKRAINE

Before The Cameras Leave Ukraine

AN ANTHOLOGY RAISING FUNDS FOR UKRAINIAN REFUGEES

Edited by Rebecca Graham

THE **BLACK SPRING**
PRESS GROUP

First published in 2023
by Eyewear Publishing Ltd.,
an imprint of Black Spring Publishing Group
United Kingdom

Introduction © Rebecca Graham
Typeset with graphic design by Edwin Smet
All rights reserved © 2023 all authors

The right of all authors to be identified as author of this work has been asserted in accordance with section 77 of the Copyright, Designs and Patents Act 1988

ISBN 978-1-915406-32-3

BLACKSPRINGPRESSGROUP.COM

PUBLISHER'S NOTE
the poems use spelling and grammar
chosen by the individual poets and have not
been standardised by one national style.

For all Refugees from War.

TABLE OF CONTENTS

9 INTRODUCTION

10 3 HAIKU
11 A HARD FROST
12 A STRAY IN THE SQUARE
13 ALONE IN THE CITY
14 BACKYARD
15 BE WARY NOW, BE WATCHFUL
17 BEFORE THE CAMERAS LEAVE UKRAINE
18 BEING A HUMAN BEING MEANS DIFFERENT THINGS TO DIFFERENT HUMAN BEINGS
19 ~~BLACKOUT~~
20 BOY/MAN/SOLDIER
21 DIGESTING WHAT'S ON THE INTERNET
22 EACH SLOW DUSK
23 EIDERDOWN
24 EMPTY DOLLHOUSES IN VALLEYS
26 FEAR
27 FERMATA
28 HOURS BEFORE
30 I USED TO READ THE NOVELS OF SVETLANA ALEXIEVICH
31 LINES
32 MARCH 6TH
34 MARCHING
35 MOSCOW IN DECEMBER
36 MURMUR
37 NABOTH'S VINEYARD 2022
39 PARLOR DRAMA
41 ROLL OF HONOUR
42 SEEDS OF WAR
43 SENT PACKING
44 SIMPLE ENDING

46	SKY DRUM
47	SUNFLOWER LAMENT
49	SWADDLED IN PATRIOTISM
50	TESTAMENT
51	THE ATHEIST'S PRAYER
52	THE BOOK OF SADNESS OPENS IN BUCHA
53	THE CHILDREN
54	THE OLD WOMAN IN ODESSA
56	THE POETS OF UKRAINE
58	THE THUMBSCREW
60	THE VIRGIN OF MARIUPOL
61	THIS SCEPTRED ISLE
62	TO THOSE WHOSE HEFTY FEET CRUSH
63	TWENTY TWENTY-TWO
64	UKRAINE DIRT, 2022
65	VIRGA
66	POETS' BIOGRAPHIES

INTRODUCTION

After the shocking invasion of Ukraine earlier this year, we at The Black Spring Press Group felt it right to announce an anthology to raise funds and help support the people impacted by the appalling violence of the war. Sixty percent of the entry fees from each author has already contributed to the cause and been donated to The Sanctuary Foundation (https://www.sanctuaryfoundation.org.uk/) which helps to house refugees from Ukraine.

It is very easy to feel slightly helpless as we watch each new challenge unfold, simultaneously seeming both a world away and yet also at our feet. It is with this in mind that I am so proud to present a collection of poems which remind us of how difficult times can often bring us back to our roots as an expressive and creative global community. It is in these times that art can bring us together and build us up when very little else seems to make a difference.

Each poem included in the anthology has been carefully selected for its strength, beauty, or resonance with the extraordinary and awful events taking place since February 2022. Some debate the relevance of poetry in our modern age – I think these are partially fuelled by an expectation to feel the 'right' way when interpreting a poem, even if you struggle to relate to its contents. Despite being a student of literature by choice, I admit that even I have often understood the Marmite effect that poetry has on people. My hope for this collection is that each poem evokes something in you, the reader, as strongly as they did in me when I selected them.

Rebecca Graham, London, December 2022
Editor

3 HAIKU
Marcus Fedder

Army boots and mud in Ukraine
The land that darkness knows
History repeating hades

...

Dasein – the essence of mankind
Fundamental existence
Undeniable and yet denied

...

Thus spoke Zarathustra
Wisdom of eternity
Like snowflakes in the rain

A HARD FROST
Deborah Harvey

They've cut back the scrub
where we might have made a den to overwinter in

and not in a tender way, they brought in
machines that churned the ground, hacked and

flailed at ashes and elder
until their trunks were bone and splinter.

The field and everything in it
is struck dumb.

We too are hurting, burnt back and stumbling
over ruts and icy clumps.

A STRAY IN THE SQUARE
Ken Evans

The streets are empty winds, no whiff
of a message in them. I lick a puddle

on the cobblestones. Meaty. Dust
everywhere and worn luggage left

in the street, as travellers rush to
a wishing-well of a departure platform.

All the barking says, 'Go', but my master
must return with sausage and take this

soft wound, stroke the spot over my eyes
while my brown head rests in his lap,

but no tidbits from under a table, no table legs
at all, their piled and twisted chrome glinting

in a corner of Nezalezhnosti Square. New beasts
trip the security lights at the blazing factory.

I snuffle away the dream of a rat as a hunchback
ogre, in my one-eyed sleep. Trains won't whistle,

children pat my shown ribs, hedges are under-
scented, as the lamps still upright, send no signals.

A constant whar-whar of white vans lifting people
into tunnels of light leaking from their back doors.

ALONE IN THE CITY
Anna O'Connor

I see a figure in the distance
His heartache reverberates around the emptiness
I can taste the pain in his loneliness

I run to him; I know he needs me
A small child, bruised, wrapped in his arms I see
My feet pound harder on the ground
So I might reach them in time
So that I too, can be found

But as I get closer, I realise
There is only anger in his eyes.
And now I see
An old man, broken by our choices
Cradling these ashes

A nation turns to dust
Look what war has done to us

BACKYARD
Dominic Dulin
after watching the Daily Show with Trevor Noah

not just in your backyard, America
do the police push a black woman
off a train and let the white person on

not just in your backyard, America
is a man from Congo told to fight
for a country he doesn't call home

not just in your backyard, America
are the police tap tapping on car windows
saying *you can't stay here*

not just in your backyard, America
does it take four long days
for Zimbabwean students to reach the Romanian border

not just in your backyard, America
are fences unmoving for Syrian refugees
but open for white Ukrainians

not just in your backyard, America
white refugees are given open arms
while black and brown refugees face teargas and guns

not just in your backyard, America
does the white Ukrainian in the U.S.
see himself in a refugee,

while the Zimbabwean tells herself
that could be me

– a refugee *too* refugee for majority white countries

BE WARY NOW, BE WATCHFUL
Anthony S. James

And now for some kind of future;
Although everything seems unhinged...
The hammer-faced present is grinning
Through the black-red blasts that shred
The fabric of the moment, the tissue of the past...
Tales of fear and bombast,
Told to justify your death,
Told in the East to fall like pellets in the West.
(And North and the South, the icecaps melt.
Even the stars will not help –
No message from across the light years;
All must be done by ourselves.)

Yet the seasons revolve and the wind is stirring,
Therefore to the task at hand!
If not intimate hope, then a stubborn existence...
On the open page of refuge in some other land.

Just as traders and priests came to Native Americans,
So the rapacious Eurasian continent fell upon you;
Pressing its iron heels into the Ukrainian earth –
Teutonic knights and Slavonic knights,
Barons and bishops and patriarchs at prayer,
Double-headed eagle, hammer and sickle,
The slick and correct SS directors of death,
The bloody-minded commissars of the bullet.
And always, always you were deceived.
Be wary now, be watchful –
As you already know so well...

Peril lies not only in the merciless sledgehammer
Of a missile falling from the spring skies,
But also in the virtual reality of dizzying money
And the dancing currency markets.
In the twisted tunnel of history, walls wet with blood,
Self-reliance alone is certain.

Beyond that there are sisters, brothers
And poets – how many poets first stirred
Like sap-laden shoots in Ukraine's air,
To be confidently claimed by other nations!
There is the blue of the sky
And the yellow-gold of laughter,
Even when the humour is bitter, bitter...
When the jokes are desperate
And come rising up from the darkness.

BEFORE THE CAMERAS LEAVE UKRAINE
Carey Taylor
a Golden Shovel after Wislawa Szymborska

They bury their dead in mass graves after
Russian troops commandeer their burial sites and as every
corpse-filled hole pools borscht-red from this war
and as 2 x 4 crosses are pushed into hard dirt after someone
has written the names of a mother and son in black sharpie, someone else has
put on thick rubber gloves then sat on body bags piled in the back of a truck pleading to
some lowercase god in bomb-blackened skies, to please, please, clean
this bloody broth up.

BEING A HUMAN BEING MEANS DIFFERENT THINGS TO DIFFERENT HUMAN BEINGS
Ma'ayan Agmon

There's a sculpture near the red square that shows the sins of the world
The sin that stands tallest is indifference –
The blurred line between killing and silence.

As a child, I was there almost every week
With my mother, asking me to take note of what life holds
               to go away from the fairy tale realm and on to the path of
my responsibilities.
She was building my moral compass.

And isn't this what being a human being is?
It seems like this sin has been forgotten
Or perhaps, people, on their way to the red square,
Never stopped by this sculpture.

~~BLACKOUT~~

Adele Evershed

War –
~~I sat down to write a poem~~
~~full of well-~~ **~~torn images~~**
~~—sunflowers under blue skies—~~ **~~mud~~** ~~sticky and black as~~
~~blood~~~~—a rabbit in the~~
~~rubble~~ ~~of a maternity hospital—~~ **~~fleeting figures~~** ~~leaving~~
~~footprints~~ **~~in the ash~~**~~—and~~
~~always the~~ **~~children~~**~~—bright as daisies—~~ **~~uprooted~~** ~~but still~~
~~singing songs~~ **~~from~~**
~~Disneyland—it's~~ **~~a small world~~** ~~after all~~
~~you know the sort of thing~~
~~yet as I stared out at the same blue sky~~
~~through the benevolent bars of leafless trees~~
~~I knew I had nothing left to say.~~
~~So~~ I took my words away.

BOY/MAN/SOLDIER
Kim Malinowski

proud behind hasty tires
piled protection, whispered
dusty prayer

his lips tight, rifle
hidden close
his grandfather's pocketknife
heft at his thigh
knows blood and dirt
childhood slides into soldier

his city burns
he starves
buildings shake
he waits
his life is to wait
live for moments
quick breeze when there is no acrid
smell of gasoline and rot
in wisp of wind
his grandmother's dabbed
perfume almost close

he knows his history
determined to play the part

DIGESTING WHAT'S ON THE INTERNET
Lara C. Widmann

white noise and tons of smoke,
while my head is in my boyfriend's lap.
resting – while hearts are crushed,
and you're running out of gas.

my wine-dark lips on skin and body parts,
and I swear I didn't spend tons of money on my dress –
there's a Lamborghini on the internet,
in midst of limbs and plastic bags.

there's two of us –
but you're facing the worst,
and I'm still here.

EACH SLOW DUSK
Rebecca Faulkner

I toss a shilling in the Serpentine
from the shallows   grey voices

of the dead frighten carp   nibbling
at the day   there is no end to it

this murmuring of hours   in my scuffed
brogues I scrawl   on yellowed envelopes

        I do not want to die

setting it down as the artillery fires   & fires
I will go mad remembering

trembling   my laces tied with pond scum
fingers clasping   vines twisted in his hair

the cadet with missing teeth   reading Keats
        while flames lick the escalator

at Regents Park tube   everyone gives up
something   & I am not afraid

to be alone   with the broken bannister
stacking clean plates neatly   after she leaves

I will open the window wide   usher in the dead from
Thessaly Flanders   Belsen & Baghdad

we will sit & watch   a girl crossing the square
in a green dress   the trees alive with nightingales

for Septimus Smith

EIDERDOWN
Catherine Swire

On your bed, a black eiderdown
with flowers, pink flowers in the night,

from my granny's island

for years it lay heaped in a boathouse
(my brother, as the boy, inherited the house
which turned out to be more trouble than it's...)

I had to wash this eiderdown of mine
at least three times (with special soap)

now it shines with flowers in the night

I like the sound its old cotton makes
and that I can share this eiderdown with you

flowers in the night

a move away...

our island.

EMPTY DOLLHOUSES IN VALLEYS
Uzomah Ugwu

Dolls left with eyes and other body parts missing
Caught by a bullet still with some sight
not enough light but the hit is felt
The start of war fills a home with injustice
No freedom, lack of peace are stuck in pillows
echoing the warm broken sleep from houses
that can no longer hold a home

The stove still hot with caution
The dining room is set,
but the family has fled,
not been fed
Brother and father now offering
more than their bodies
For their country
A mother runs down

her husband so he will
never forget what he meant to her.
One last kiss, locked in each other's eyes as one
becomes a freedom fighter and the other a refugee of war
Overcrowded trains, buses dodging bullets
and bombs in every direction
No use for a map. Traveling in mass disaster
more deserted homes
Lost her family under siege, locked in a stare
with abandoned animals
Curtain calls on stages that are outperformed
by nameless soldiers marching on scattered soil

Heard bombs by her window, saw her dolls
shake while under covers aching for her country
No longer able to embrace her innocence
she grabs onto war and runs

FEAR
Jane Lamb

as the sirens sound
with hearts beating fast
we wait underground

our nerves tightly wound
dark thoughts flashing past
as the sirens sound

wild rumours abound
pale faced and aghast
we wait underground

what hope's to be found
in the enemy's blast
as the sirens sound?

will our land rebound
will peace come at last?
we wait underground
as the sirens sound

FERMATA
Breda Joyce

Under the portico of the train station at Lviv
a piano gives shelter. It's four degrees below
but Karpenko's freezing fingers glide over the keys.
He continues to play as more refugees arrive.

Like Moses, he strikes against the hardened face
of war, releases a cascade of notes that takes them
to a source below the sound. They stop and listen,
cling to one another, are taken

where no sirens scream, where the sky's
still blue and clear. Karpenko's fingers
grow warmer; his grace notes hold them
in these moments between ivory and black.

HOURS BEFORE
Scott Hobbs Bourne

An incredible tune
From my youth
Church bells calling out
Hour or event

A slow moving
Thunder storm
Grumbles out into
The afternoon
The sky grows dark
As dry lightning
Twists above the trees
Reversed skin in sky
Varicose veins
Stretch out white
Over blue body
Giving birth to occasional drop
It will be hours before it starts
And hours before it stops

A loud pitter patter
Over the lawn and street
Coming towards me
That does not give-way
Till late in the evening

A blind/deaf rain
Free of thunder or lightning
A mute whore

That screams rape
Although she is warm and wet

Two large moths
Fly around under a streetlamp
In some sort of
Suicidal mating dance
Until
One is hit
And gracelessly flutters to the ground
It takes slightly longer
For its desperate lover
But soon she too
Is struck
And falls to the street like her love

I USED TO READ THE NOVELS OF SVETLANA ALEXIEVICH
Jesse Albatrosov

I used to read the novels of
Svetlana Alexievich;
memories from the mouths
of children, feelings watered
down in English. Their mothers,
fathers, brothers, sisters dug pits
with their hands, stood at the
edges facing Germans,
bodies weak armor for bullets –
the need to run and hide, find new
mamas and papas pumping through
adolescent, prepubescent veins.
I saw these memories in black and white –
imagined lived lives beyond them
new memories to pack old wounds,
book pages turn on a lived horror
we learn about so it does not repeat again.
But Ukraine's photos are in color, moving pictures,
and the descent into a grave remains the same.

LINES
A.C. Clarke

Queuing at checkpoints, riverbanks,
on the cold shores of Calais;
under freezing rain, under searing winds, under hail
of bullets;
speaking many languages, but all
speaking the language of pain.

Lines ruled on maps
to cross with tanks
to cross with hardwon papers
to cross with nothing more
than a lucky prayer.

What if like birds riding free air
we flowed with currents and windshifts?

What if we let differences mingle
like coloured threads in a pattern
where each is itself
each woven into the rest?

What if, citizens of everywhere,
we joined protective hands to circle
the whole round world
our one, our only earth?

MARCH 6TH
Christopher M. James

1
A man's full hand
flat on the window
fingers apart
to eat space.

When pulled away
there's a tiny hand
the other side
reciprocating.

And behind it
a small face, *sfumato*,
fading in the shadow
of the carriage.

2
They know who they are
and the yellow armband
is a betrothal, a
gold ring for the marriage
of their entire bodies
at a sudden altar.

3
Before,
the Kyiv dam raised
the Dnieper water level.
The Irpin had to be pumped

to run its course there:
a river flowing upwards...
A stream of people passes from
one military arm to the next,
an improvised charm bracelet,
one wheeling a suitcase
one pushing a pram along
the middle-finger wreck
of the bridge.

4
Essential supplies
overflow at fine-line borders:
the world on the edge
of hunger.

5
We've carefully trowelled
our heartfelt lives
and what have we learned?
The irregularity of surfaces:
how a single, isolated mind
becomes an incommensurate
jackhammer.

MARCHING
M. Chambers

You weren't there as we gathered around the Cross.
The Ukrainian flag on your Facebook page
but no boots on the ground.
You weren't there
while we carried flags and Sunflowers,
too busy creating your latest meme;
clapping for victory.
You weren't there while we decorated the shutters
with symbols of shame.
Perhaps ashamed yourself that you didn't care that much,
and you might get in trouble with the Police
and anyway,
it would never happen here.
We walked home in our European shroud.
A most terrible sound.
Silence.

MOSCOW IN DECEMBER
Ijen Kim
(Moscow, December 2014)

When days grow dark
When neon red that flecks the wintered street
And what were ruby drops now look like neighbour's blood
The city signs, their numbers gleam and grow
That woman with a wheelbarrow full of cash for bread
Old schoolbook picture fallen from my head
The sun that fled and pale stingy light
I knew it here just nature's resting time
Not real night
Then came the months of bitter seeds
Now falling rain, the neon spots and stains
Strangely echo nearby bombs and flames
When days stay dark
And hard to find a smile, gift or hopeful hint
Dawn's brief hand still reaches tender fingers through the sky
And strokes the snow with short-lived blush
And sets the puddle gems aglow
It's not my place to cry
But rather thank for eyes that see
And heart that's glad of small rewards
When days seem drained of all that made them bright
To catch the early morning moon
The blots of blue between the clouds
Is comforter and tears dried

MURMUR
Roy Canning

That summer the birds
were given new names

the damselfly became
the grey, neat young girl

the bearded tit,
the moustached reed-worker

the rose finch, red creature
of the briar

they are not allowed
to use their old names

or take part in unlawful
gatherings

nor play peek-a-boo
in the reeds

spider webs and twigs weave
the fibres of their nests

in tunnels as deep
as tombs

that summer chirping
was banned

and they renamed the sun
and called it the moon

NABOTH'S VINEYARD 2022
Stan Galloway

Let me have your vineyard to use for a vegetable garden, since it is close to my palace.
— 1 Kings 21.2 [NIV]

   Ahab
From the top of my tower
it is an eyesore
to see someone comfortable
without my permission.

The ease of kings is the obvious desire of the people.

If you are happy
you must be blaspheming
  must be a drunken Jew
  who hunts down Jews
  traitor to kin and decency.

I'll plow up your grapes
to grow beets for my borscht.
I'll do the plowing, no worries,
you just vacate –
or be plowed under.

   Naboth
God forbid that I should give to you
the land of my ancestors
generations of proud men
even under Samaritan yokes.

I am a simple man, but free.

My wine has slaked entire cities
                eased their aches each evening
                granted rest to weary bones.
I do not need your beets
                your plow.
Now, go –
before I sick the dogs on you.

PARLOR DRAMA
David Radavich

A Perspective from Inside

We are not allowed
to call this a war.

So I will call it
a parlor drama

written by a dark Russian
whose memory is
faulty and dangerous.

An author of both
cruelty and absurdity

on a world-wide stage
that does not applaud.

The bombing of a maternity
hospital, the shooting
of beggars in a bread line
are not tragedy

but the successful
perpetration of a strategy.

Now he has put his name
on an era as he wished.

The play will be forever
done. It will have many acts.

And the parlor will be long
destroyed in the minds of men.

ROLL OF HONOUR
David Howard

Memories are not important
letters brought to the front counter, they are more
like those name-tags torn from clothes...

I see skyscrapers as war memorials:
all those people, gone without turning
off the lights.

SEEDS OF WAR
Ralph La Rosa

Seeds stolen by their comrade Stalin
a century ago have kin
in Ukraine: now as steel artillery blows
by Russia's swarming orcs to starve them,
raping the land and stealing their freedom.
Will Putin reap what he now sows?

Note: Stalin's adopted surname means steel. Ukrainians call the invaders orcs, after brutal humanoid monsters created by Tolkien.

SENT PACKING
Kay Ritchie

bundled   off
bundle   clutched
each kilometre   *stop!*   then *go!*
divides them from before and what they knew
but still they drag their pulled up roots &
pray for welcome somewhere
where people can't pronounce their name &
they won't know the name for
journey   yearning   fear   new year   or love

SIMPLE ENDING
Vincent Casaregola

This time, shame to tell,
it is the world's end, but
not as we had expected
nor envisioned in some
dark fantasy of artful doom.

It is unassuming and
unassumed, unnoticed by
the great and wise,
unnoticed by the fools
as well – just another warm
day in a false spring.

It begins simply, like
a machine wearing down,
like a friendship grown cold
after too many years
of distance and no desire.

Something falls out of joint,
and something else, out of orbit,
and there you have it – apocalypse
in a nutshell, the simplified form.

Someone is trying to catch up
on the mail and the bills,
someone is rushing to work,
anticipating an angry boss,
someone is late dropping

kids at pre-school – the normal
routines will unravel presently.

Somewhere, a lover – man or
woman – waits at a table,
clutching a coffee cup, feeling
warmth soothing the hands,
while behind the tinted lenses
eyes stare into space, anticipating
a beloved about to arrive
in a rush of apologies and embracing,
and, holding that thought, just as
the dust begins to dance
across the tiles, sees the sky
descend, without even a shout.

SKY DRUM
You Mingna

In black spring we go on picking
And pick a basketful of shepherd's purse

The feathers shedding are a fall of mother's ashes
A collectivity doesn't read a closed elegiac address

Distance is wind-coat of loneliness
Wind is hunter middleman

The reversed teeth of butterfly
A thirteen-hour river is running to

Alert dreams. What time is it
When it's shuddering in bloodied red?

The moon that cannot close the eyes
Cannot see the clenched fingers of a baby

And the fool holding me tight

SUNFLOWER LAMENT
Elizabeth Carey

Hearts ache for a world that was,
tears flow for all who feel loss.

Souls wail for order to return,
minds seek answers as towns burn.

The rich hide in their ivory towers,
as people shelter 'neath earth and cower.

The futility of war has never been learnt,
tyrants seek more – fully hellbent.

Displaced families flee from it all,
as they see their homes topple and fall.

Vacant faces, chaos, as they look to the sky,
national pride, dignity, still heads held high.

Cities flattened – spirits soar higher,
courage, determination 'gainst enemy fire.

Diplomacy from leaders around the world
is not stopping this foe as atrocities unfurl.

His time will come to face all that he's done,
what will be left of this nation, its sons?

Farmlands destroyed, their crops no more,
cities on fire, the enemy at the door.

Let sunflowers flourish in our gardens this year,
a salute to those who live in fear.

Let the world embrace those who've run,
nurture them, love them until they return.

Let peace be restored to this brave land
as Ukrainians unite to make a stand.

SWADDLED IN PATRIOTISM
Dr. Deidra Suwanee Dees

Excerpt from 'Indian Ice: Indigenous Witness / Estv-Cate' Het'ute'

they celebrate
a day off from work and school
– swaddled in patriotism,
        the heralded navigator
        and renowned explorer;

sitting alone
        I know your exploits of
        countless Christian sins –
stealer of land and children,
cold slave owner,

building your house on the
        blood of natives,
filling your hunger on the
nectar of virgins –
        clumsy navigator,
        crucible murderer –

come close to me
        and smell my nectar,
        rub your hand
against my nipple,
        cast your
        finger below my navel,

Mr. Columbus, let me whisper,
        come closer to me;
my breath like fire
        erases your existence
when I whisper
Genocide

TESTAMENT
A.Z. Foreman

Translated from the Ukrainian of Taras Shevchenko, written in 1845

When I die, then bury me
On a rolling plain.
Raise my barrow in the soil
Of my dear Ukraine
With the wheatfields and the cliffs
Of a plunging shore
In my sight, where I can hear
The booming Dnipro's roar.

When its seaward waters bear
The invaders' blood
From Ukraine, then I will leave
Field and hill for good.
I will quit it all and fly
Bursting up to God
And say prayers... but till then
I don't know a god.

Bury me then rise again
And shatter your chains.
Stand and water freedom with
Blood from tyrant veins.
Then in a new family,
The great kin of the free,
Say a kindly, quiet word
In my memory.

THE ATHEIST'S PRAYER
Annie Percik

The moon in the sky
On a bright summer's day
Brings new meaning to insignificance
The trees do not know
The troubles of men
Who go walking beneath their indifference

Time passes on
Inexorable still
And my life here will not be remembered
It comforts me now
That obscurity beckons
The achievements I will have engendered

THE BOOK OF SADNESS OPENS IN BUCHA
Nicole Yurcaba

The Book of Sadness opens in Bucha:
grief   despair
        absence of hope
bombed cars
a single keychain held
        by blackened fingers
a bike overturned
        the rider facedown

The World said, 'Never again'.

Then, it looked away.
Then, the soldiers found ashes in Mariupol
    the missiles struck a train station in Kramatorsk
        a little boy lies on a bench   his arm hanging limp
                                                        his open wide eyes
        pleading *Why?*

THE CHILDREN
Geoff Yorath

They are clutching teddies and dolls
And shuffling past trains
Under a station canopy
In a foreign country.
They carry small bundles,
Fumble for explanations.
You can see in their eyes that
Something has been left behind
In bombed out homes and kindergartens.
On a platform far from home
Innocence and experience meet
And shuffle past each other.

THE OLD WOMAN IN ODESSA
Diana Woodcock

The old woman in Odessa says
she will stay, she will not be driven away.
Gardening, she smiles as she proclaims
>Spring has come again,
>the flowers will bloom.

This isn't about gloom and doom.
She's seen it all before, only then
Russia was the savior, World War II.
Now she's turned enemy.
>Never mind, won't you
>join me for a cup of tea?

She says if the day arrives when she's
dragged away by her well-meaning
family, she'll be ready to go, although
unwillingly. Her small bag is packed
with food and a blanket for her cat.
>But for now, the snow melted
>and spring in the air, I will not sing
>a song of despair. Though every-
>thing elsewhere's gone grey,
>the flowers in my garden will bloom.

The old woman from Odessa is carried
away by her faith in Mother Nature –
she is nurtured. The bombs are falling on
homes and hospitals, schools and gardens.
Look there – the vets are treating people's
pets in a bombed out animal hospital.

All night the woman from Odessa speaks
to me, breaking the silence. And I listen,
having turned away from the grim,
late-breaking news. She upstages them
all, so I dedicate pages to her. I prefer
her version of how it all will turn out.

> *The flowers will bloom again*
> *in my garden in Odessa.*
> *No madman can stop them.*

THE POETS OF UKRAINE
Kendall Bradley

As their elegant cities
incomprehensibly burn
and explode into rubble,
as young girls lie in pools
of blood on the once
tree-lined streets, the
poets of Ukraine arm
themselves with shotguns
and deer rifles and
unrelenting courage.

Though they know the
pen is mightier than
the sword, their poems
now are the orange
blossoms of Molotov
cocktails and the deadly
trace of stingers seeking
their marks.

In this unhappy hour,
all Ukrainians are poets
as the cadence and meter
of their lives are odes to
the best the human spirit
can offer, yet still, we in
America can but watch
aghast and in helpless
horror as they struggle

and die in the barbarous
prosody of war.

Though we would not
have it so, we hear the
poets of Ukraine with
impotent ears, we watch
their travails with impotent
eyes, we plant sunflowers
and water them with our
tears to no avail, except
perhaps that we may weep
away just enough of our
own unpoetic, speechless
guilt.

THE THUMBSCREW
Jeremy Grant

You bring him in
and tie him to the chair.
You don't know what he's done
but you're going to find out,
even if it kills him.
When you hold his arm
to attach the screw,
he writhes like a fish.
The anticipation of torture
is torture – it's true.
You turn the screw
and he thrashes in your arms.
You turn it again
and he bucks the weight
of your body from the ground.
You cup your ear
and wait for the words,
but the words don't come.
You turn it again,
as if the thresholds of pain
were indeed infinite.
Why some of the audience
stand and hurl
abuse at the stage
is simply beyond you.
You embrace him tenderly
and whisper in his ear,
then turn it again.
The audience watch.

They are mesmerised –
fixed to their seats.
They cover their eyes.
Some of them weep.
One of them faints.
The place is in uproar.
You keep turning
until he talks.

THE VIRGIN OF MARIUPOL
Alexa Poteet

Of course at the outset,
she was not.
But who could deny
her invisible nimbus,

tri-radiance. The look
of knowing god –
ghost grey, elusive
as smoke.

Against the icebergs
of broken concrete, the flaming
yellow vests of the rescuers,
she spilled

a vivd pink, across the black
polka dotted blanket. Inappropriate
as watermelon
or strawberries, a ripeness

only for summer hours
not this snow,
(or was it embers?)
in reverse falling up.

THIS SCEPTRED ISLE
Kelly Davis

The first day
the hosting website went live
100,000 people signed up,
opening their hearts and homes
to Ukrainian refugees.

In the same country
whose government
refuses safe passage
for Syrians and Afghans
who drown in the English Channel.

TO THOSE WHOSE HEFTY FEET CRUSH
Danylo Onyshchenko

        To   those   whose hefty feet crush   мир:*

    who   **break**   objects, and other living things

                series of large origami creatures
            products of colonialism

we sat in the sun on   the beach

we   find new ways to listen

                            and
              imagine and realize more

just and better worlds.

                                     *мир: peace

TWENTY TWENTY-TWO
Joel Scarfe

By the trembling water's edge
beneath the blink of darkening trees
in a plagiarism of storm
stands this hapless year

forlorn and already weary
of what it has been forced to bear
in its arms – a tally of official lies,
a sermon from the front line.

In a thousand years some respected tome
of history will plot this time
coherently – as if coherence, as if reason
had never been renounced.

UKRAINE DIRT, 2022
Casey Hampton

On television you see, there
dogs yelping broken, jagged
sounds like people make when
whole buildings stop being anything
more than a space for memory. Rubble
framed on television, so convenient
advertisements for life insurance, reverse
mortgages and larger closets allow us time,
and here's when we sprint with immediacy
to the bathroom that smells like cut flowers
and soap we bought last week. We wash our hands
because we are civilized beings and have time
to swallow filtered water as our flatscreens
made in China. Currently, Breaking
News is the new interruption
we try to overlook, we truly believe valiantly
how brave those people are asking for our help.

VIRGA
David Francis

I have read that mourning, by its gradual toil,
its indescribable burden,
slowly erases pain. I do not believe,
cannot believe,
that proposition. For me, time only dilutes
the emotion of loss, does not expunge it.
Though I no longer weep,
what is motionless
what is held in distant murmurs
comes to meet me.
What I have lost is not
the abundance of a past,
but a being.
Not a being, a quality of being.
Not the indispensable
but the irreplaceable –
plays of sunlight,
individual flames of a fire,
the honeycomb of smiles,
each flake of snow
that has fallen in Ukraine.
What remains
is absolute, unqualifiable,
rods of rain or sleet or ice
that trail from clouds
and never reach the ground
or find the edge of certainty,
never heal the breach between
heaven and earth

POETS' BIOGRAPHIES

MA'AYAN AGMON
Ma'ayan Agmon is an IB teacher, spoken-word poetry guide and co-founder of an Israeli rap group. She writes for *Matok Ve Mar*, with poems and short stories published in journals including *Lekol Ha Ruhot*. She performs in Poetry Slam events. She holds a Bachelor's from Tel Aviv University and is working on her Master's.

JESSE ALBATROSOV
Jesse Albatrosov is an American poet studying a Master's of Fine Art in poetry and literary translation at Vermont College of Fine Arts. A 2018 Pushcart Prize nominee and Button Poetry chapbook semifinalist, her work features in *The American Journal of Poetry*, *Allegory Ridge*, and Press 53's *Prime Number Magazine*.

SCOTT HOBBS BOURNE
Scott Hobbs Bourne lives in Paris. He has published a novel, several journals, and a poem trilogy. His poetry was put to score by American composer Shinji Eshima. His short stories were nominated for the 2016 American Library in Paris Book Award. Recent work includes an illustrated book of poems for children.

KENDALL COLLINS BRADLEY
Kendall Collins Bradley lives on the Eastern Shore of Virginia in the United States. He holds Bachelor's and Master's degrees from the University of Virginia where he first began to write verse. He is the author of five books of poetry.

ROY CANNING
Roy Canning is a poet and writer from Dundee. He gained a PhD in Education from Aberdeen University and lives in Scotland. He has been published in poetry anthologies and pamphlets and given readings at Dundee Literary Festival and Being Human International Festival.

ELIZABETH ANNE CAREY
Elizabeth Anne Carey is almost 75 years young and has been writing poems and short stories for many years, though only sharing her work for two. She has been recently published in *Hooded* by Crowvus and in an upcoming anthology, *Dreich*.

VINCENT CASAREGOLA
Vincent Casaregola teaches American literature and film, creative writing, and rhetorical studies at Saint Louis University. He has published poetry in a number of journals, including *2River*, *The Bellevue Literary Review*, *Blood and Thunder*, and *Dappled Things*. He has also published creative nonfiction in *New Letters* and *The North American Review*.

M. CHAMBERS
Born in 1956, M. Chambers' working life was spent as an archaeologist, but he has retired to the North York Moors. His short stories have won prizes with the Federation of Writers (Scotland) and Luna Press, and been long and shortlisted. His poetry has appeared in *Lucent Dreaming* and anthologies.

A.C. CLARKE
A.C. Clarke has published five full poetry collections and six pamphlets. She was a winner in the Cinnamon Press 2017 pamphlet competition and has twice won the Second Light Long Poem competition. Her pamphlet, *Wedding Grief*, centred on the marriage of Paul and Gala Éluard, was published in 2021.

KELLY DAVIS

Kelly Davis lives in Cumbria working as a freelance editor. Her poetry has been published in magazines including *Mslexia*, *Magma* and *Shooter*. She appears in the Black Spring Press *Best New British and Irish Poets 2019–2021* anthology, and she has twice been shortlisted for the Aesthetica Creative Writing Award.

DOMINIC DULIN

Dominic Dulin is a poet and musician from Cleveland, currently studying in the Northeast Ohio Master of Fine Arts graduate programme at Cleveland State University. He has had poetry published by *Modern Haiku Magazine*, *Surreal Poetics*, *Frogpond Journal*, and *Bones Haiku Journal*. His work tends to focus on experimental poetry, surrealism and haiku.

KEN EVANS

Ken Evans' poetry appears in *Poetry Scotland*, *Magma*, and elsewhere. He won the Kent & Sussex Poetry competition in 2018 and his second collection, *To An Occupier Burning Holes*, is forthcoming. His first was from Eyewear.

ADELE EVERSHED

Adele Evershed was born in Wales, and lived in Hong Kong and Singapore before settling in Connecticut. Adele started out writing scripts for a theatre group. Since then, her work has been published in over eighty journals and anthologies. Finishing Line Press will publish her first chapbook, *Turbulence in Small Spaces*, next year.

REBECCA FAULKNER

Rebecca Faulkner is a London-born poet and arts educator based in Brooklyn. She won the *Sand Hills Literary Magazine* National

Poetry Contest and Prometheus Unbound Poetry Competition. She holds a Bachelor's in English Literature and Theatre Studies from the University of Leeds, and a PhD from the University of London. Her debut poetry collection will be published in 2023.

MARCUS FEDDER

After decades in London and Shanghai, Marcus lives in the Swiss mountains, keeping busy with several work endeavours, alongside painting and writing. His first novel, *Sarabande*, was published in 2008; his second, *German Justice*, in 2020. Marcus holds a PhD in International Relations. His art supports Children of the Mekong.

A.Z. FOREMAN

A.Z. Foreman is a poet, literary and finance translator, and language teacher. He has a Bachelor's in Linguistics from the University of Chicago and Master's in Arabic Language from the University of Maryland. He is completing a PhD at Ohio State University. His work featured in *Jerkpoet*, *Asymptote*, *Metamporphoses* and one BBC radio broadcast.

DAVID FRANCIS

David Francis lives in Melbourne, working as a transplant surgeon, and has published his varied writings in international and Australian journals and anthologies. His first poetry collection was published by the *Melbourne Poets Union* in 2013. He holds a PhD in Creative Writing from the University of Melbourne.

STAN GALLOWAY

Stan Galloway is the founder of Pier-Glass Poetry and the Bridgewater International Poetry Festival. He is the author/editor of nine collections of poetry, including *Endlessly Rocking* (Unbound Content, 2019).

JEREMY GRANT

Jeremy Grant lives with his family in Leicestershire and teaches at a local sixth form college. His poetry has appeared in *Anima, Magma, Poetry Nottingham, The Journal, The Coffee House, The French Literary Review, The Emma Press Anthology of Fatherhood,* and *War, Literature, and the Arts.*

CASEY HAMPTON

Casey Hampton is a sight-impaired author and poet from Oregon, born in 1974. He graduated from Lindenwood University with a Master's of Fine Art in Creative Writing in 2017 and is living and writing in the verdant Pacific Northwest. His poetry and fiction have appeared in numerous journals and international anthologies.

DEBORAH HARVEY

Deborah Harvey is co-Director of the Leaping Word poetry consultancy, providing writing and editorial advice, and counselling support for writers exploring personal material in their work. Her recent poetry collection, *Learning Finity*, was published in March this year. She has also published four other collections and a historical novel.

DAVID HOWARD

New Zealander David Howard is the author of *Rāwaho: the Completed Poems* and editor of *A Place To Go On From: the Collected Poems of Iain Lonie*. He held the Robert Burns Fellowship at Otago University, the Prague UNESCO City of Literature Residency, and the Ulyanovsk UNESCO City of Literature Residency.

ANTHONY S. JAMES

Anthony S. James is from Wales and graduated in English and Philosophy at Swansea University. His stories, essays, poems

and reviews have been published in many journals in the UK
and Europe. His story, *The Priest and the Wind*, was translated into
Arabic for an anthology of Welsh stories in 2013.

CHRISTOPHER M. JAMES

Christopher M. James is originally from Oxfordshire. He studied
English, Philosophy and Linguistics at university. He has been
published in many poetry magazines including *Magma*, *Orbis*,
Dream Catcher, *London Grip*, and has been widely anthologised. He
has also been a prize-winner in several poetry competitions. He
lives in the Dordogne.

BREDA JOYCE

Breda Joyce's poetry has won, or been shortlisted for, several
awards and appears in anthologies and journals including *Poems
for Pandemia* and *The Best New British and Irish Poets Anthology 2019-
2021*. Her poem, *Funeral Shoes*, was featured in *The Irish Times* this
year. Her first poetry collection, *Reshaping the Light*, is recently
published.

IJEN KIM

Ijen Kim, born 1971, is a Vienna-based author, artist, and poet.
She studied conference interpreting in Paris and has worked as
an interpreter, translator, and journalist. Moscow was her long-
time home. She has three published novels, *The Snuff Bottle Boy*
and *The Sunset Emperor* in English, and *Poyezed Trotskogo* in Russian.

JANE LAMB

Jane Lamb is retired, living in Glasgow, has been writing poetry
for several years and is a member of the Glasgow Readers
and Writers group. She is a member of the Federation of
Writers Scotland and has had a poem published in two of their
anthologies and others in *Dreich* magazine.

KIM MALINOWSKI
Kim Malinowski is the author of the collection *Home* and two verse novels, *Clutching Narcissus* and *Phantom Reflection*. She has two full-length books forthcoming. She was nominated for the 2022 Rhysling Award.

YOU MINGNA
Born in Chongqing, China, You Mingna is a poet, translator, and adwoman. She has a Bachelor's degree in International Economics and Trade from Chongqing University of Technology. Following her degree, she turned to a long-term self-education in philosophy and poetry. She has written a short-story collection, some poems, and essays.

ANNA O'CONNOR
Anna O'Connor is a poet and short story writer who lives in Cornwall. She is a mother of two who has previously been published in anthologies such as *Warriors Voice*, part of the Mother Light mini-series.

DANYLO ONYSHCHENKO
Danylo Onyshchenko is a Ukrainian product management student living in Berlin. He grew up in Oleksandrivka, a village in Ukraine. The piece was written due to heavy emotions aroused by the war in his home country.

ANNIE PERCIK
Annie Percik lives in London, writing novels and short stories, whilst working as a freelance editor. She has a blog about writing on her website, where all her current publications are listed, including her novels *The Defiant Spark* and *A Spectrum of Heroes*. She also hosts a media review podcast.

ALEXA POTEET
Alexa Poteet, a poet from Washington DC, holds a Master's in Poetry from Johns Hopkins University. Appearances include *Reed Magazine*, *PennUnion*, and *Sixfold*. She was a SUNYvs.SUNY's 2015 Paumanok Poetry Award semi-finalist, 2012 Pushcart Prize nominee and won Lines + Stars' 2018 Mid-Atlantic Chapbook contest. Her first pamphlet was published in 2019.

DAVID RADAVICH
David Radavich's paternal grandparents emigrated after World War I from what is now Belarus. His poetry collections include two epics, *America Bound* and *America Abroad*, *Middle East Mezze* and *The Countries We Live In*. His latest book is *Unter der Sonne/Under the Sun: German and English poems*.

KAY RITCHIE
Kay Ritchie has lived in London, Spain and Portugal, worked as a freelance photographer and radio producer, and has been published in a variety of anthologies, journals & websites. Currently living in Glasgow, her poems have appeared on windows, a Glasgow's Pollock Park installation, and a Historic Scotland film.

RALPH LA ROSA
For a year, Ralph La Rosa taught at Tbilisi State University in Soviet Georgia. He has published prose on major American writers and published short fiction, poetry, and film scripts. Now, he writes poetry, appearing online, in print journals and anthologies. His work includes *Sonnet Stanzas*, *Ghost Trees* and *My Miscellaneous Muse*.

JOEL SCARFE

Joel Scarfe is widely published. His poems feature internationally in magazines, periodicals, and anthologies. He lives in Bristol with Danish ceramicist Rebecca Edelmann and their two children.

DR. DEIDRA SUWANEE DEES

Dr. Deidra Suwanee Dees' family descend from Hotvlklke (Wind Clan) and follow Muscogee stompdance traditions. She is Director/Tribal Archivist at Poarch Band of Creek Indians in Alabama. A Cornell and Harvard graduate, she teaches Native American Studies at University of South Alabama. Her second book, *Indian Ice: Indigenous Witness/Estv-Cate' Het'ute*, is forthcoming.

CATHERINE SWIRE

Catherine Swire is a poet based in the West Midlands. She graduated from Oxford University in English. Her debut poetry collection *Soil*, published in 2021, explores how trauma is changed by landscape. It featured on Radio 4's Ramblings and at the Ledbury Poetry Festival. She teaches Catch-Up English, Creative Writing and poetry workshops.

CAREY TAYLOR

Carey Taylor is the author of *The Lure of Impermanence* (Cirque Press, 2018). She is a Pushcart Prize nominee and winner of the 2022 Neahkahnie Mountain Poetry Prize. Her work has been published in Ireland and the United States. She holds a Master's degree in School Counseling and lives in Portland.

UZOMAH UGWU

Uzomah Ugwu is a multi-disciplined artist. Her poetry, writing, and art have been featured internationally in various publications, galleries, and art spaces. She is a political, social, and cultural activist. Her core focus is on human rights, mental health, animal rights, and the rights of LGBTQIA persons.

LARA C. WIDMANN
Lara C. Widmann is a writer from Munich, born in 1997. She is about to graduate from Ludwig-Maximilians University with a Bachelor's in German philology and modern languages. Last year she was an exchange student at the University of Exeter where she studied English and creative writing. She lives in Munich.

DIANA WOODCOCK
Diana Woodcock's latest poetry collection, *Facing Aridity* (Homebound Publications), was a 2020 Prism Prize for Climate Literature finalist. Forthcoming in 2023 is *Holy Sparks*, a 2020 Paraclete Press Poetry Award finalist. Currently teaching at VCUarts Qatar, she holds a PhD in Creative Writing from Lancaster University.

GEOFF YORATH
Geoff Yorath is a retired social worker who lives near Bath and Bristol. He worked in the charity sector supporting children and parents to overcome trauma. This experience resonated with television images of refugee children in Ukraine, to become the subject of a number of his poems.

NICOLE YURCABA
Nicole Yurcaba is a Ukrainian-American poet and essayist. Her work features in journals including *The Atlanta Review*, *The Lindenwood Review*, *Whiskey Island*, *Raven Chronicles*, *West Trade Review*, *Appalachian Heritage*, and *North of Oxford*. Nicole holds a Master's of Fine Arts in Writing from Lindenwood University, teaches poetry workshops and works as a career counselor.

REBECCA GRAHAM

Rebecca Graham, born in Newcastle, is a freelance editor, writer, and an English Literature graduate from the University of Liverpool. She currently lives in Liverpool, working with the Liverpool School of Tropical Medicine.

Lightning Source UK Ltd.
Milton Keynes UK
UKHW042335220223
417418UK00005B/83